Varying States of Grace

Ian Stephen

at Pittenweem 97.

Varying States of Grace

Ian Stephen

Polygon
EDINBURGH

© Ian Stephen 1989
Polygon
22 George Square, Edinburgh

Set in Linotron Sabon
by Koinonia, Bury, and
printed and bound in
Great Britain by
Bell & Bain Ltd, Glasgow

British Library Cataloguing in
Publication Data
Stephen, Ian, 1955–
Varying states of grace.
I. Title
821'.914

ISBN 0 7486 6038 0

I would like to thank many people who encouraged,
criticised or otherwise helped me make this book.

Particularly:

Norman Malcolm Macdonald

Graeme Roberts, Matthew P McDiarmid, Thomas Crawford,
Isobel Murray – and all involved in writing groups at
Aberdeen University

Jeremy and Denise Fox, Cambo les Bains, Pays Basque

Barbara Ziehm

An Lanntair, Stornoway

and most of all my father, John Burns Stephen

ACKNOWLEDGEMENTS

Aether; Baha'i Studies, Canada; Briggistane; Cencrastus; Chapman; Dream; The Glasgow Magazine; Kunapipi (Denmark); *Lines Review; London Magazine; New Edinburgh Review; Northern Light; Poetry Canada Review; Open Space; Orbis; Tangier; Waves*(Canada); *World Order* (U.S.); *2 plus 2* (Switzerland)

Radio Scotland; Radio Forth; Radio Clyde; Northsound; Grampian TV.

Several poems were included in *Spoken* (Shelta, Edinburgh 1981)

Also on *Fathoms and Metres* (cassette-tape, with music by Alchemy, available from Croft Recordings, Tong Studio, Isle of Lewis)

11 poems from the Poems for B.Z. sequence were first published in *Poetry Australia,* 1984

'Providence' and 'Mooring' are from an exhibition of poems with Cibachrome prints originated by the *An Lanntair* gallery, Stornoway 1987 and available for hire from *An Lanntair*, Town Hall, South Beach Street, Stornoway.

CONTENTS

I. PROVISIONS
Under the Pier   13
Smoke   14
Provisions   15
Workshop   16
Fraserburgh   17
Byname   18
Kitchen-Garden   19
News Broken   19
Thrush by Water   20
End of Path   20

II. SITUATIONS
Annunciation   23
The Prince of Wales   24
One a.m.   24
Andrew   25
Station Cafeteria   26
Jeannie Robertson Memorial Concert   27
For Those who Came Soon   28
Buddha   29
Therapist, Zurich   30
Flashback   31
In the Coffee Pot   33

III. GOING NORTH
North of Norway   37
In Reykjavik   38
Below   39
Ridge Above Lake Myvatn   39
Cliffs at Neskupstadur   40
Wyre to Rousay   41

7

Sanday Island   42
Gunsights at Sanday   43
Scapa Shore   44

IV. VARYING STATES OF GRACE
St Malo   47
Sanctuary   47
Borderlands   48
          i.   Mondarrain
          ii   Contrabandier
          iii. Carcase
          iv.   Frontier
          v.   Debris
          vi.   Pic Gora Makil
Pic Du Midi D'Ossau   51
Sheltering   52
Ainhoa   53
Echaler   53
Objet Trouvé   54
Juxtaposition   55
Estuary at Bayonne   56
In Bayonne Cathedral   57
In St Jean de Luz   59

V. POEMS FOR BARBARA ZIEHM
Mushrooms   63
Shoulder   64
Ends of Roads   64
Providence   65
Stranding   66
Upper Redds   67
A858   68
Influence   69
Last Week   70
Embankment   71

Kevelaer	72
Die Alster	73
Carp-Ponds	73
Walk	74
Boat by Pier	75
Elbe	75
Bullenhuser Damm	76
Undercurrents	78
Now I Know	80

VI. GOING SOUTH

Going South	83
Gallery Talk	84
In the West End Hotel	85
In Oxford	87
Motorway Stop	88
Engraver, Mudeford	89
Royal Victoria Hospital, Boscombe	90
For Sean David	91
For my Mother	92
Shotts, 1985	93

VII. SKYLINE

Skyline	97
January 9th	98
Anton	99
Am Bord	
Walk after Breakfast	100
For Calum Tent	101
They Kill Sheep	102
Cambers	104
Circumambulation	106
Moons	107
Returning from Sròn Dìobadail	108
Mooring	109

Kingfisher
The Alter
Easy Words
...ia
...ly Thorn
Blue
Holland...er Datum
Understanding...
Now I Know

To GOOD TOMMY
Gentle Song
Gentle...le
in the West End Hotel
and...
Sleep is a Song
Leopard Man about
Rhythm come Hospital, Ascribe
For...a David
For me a Motta
...

...
Skyline
...man Web
Anon
...in Berg
Walk after the Rain
Born anni Tear
They Killed are
...inabet
Communication famon
Anon
responding from Eva Dhonard
Meeting

I
PROVISIONS

UNDER THE PIER

It was a green world we went in, under the pier.
Up there above, the dockers caught ropes
and metal boxes that had been tied to lorries
swung over the pier with vegetables and fridges
and wool and chocolate biscuits.

We never walked when we went under but
chased a way down ladders of weedy metal
and then leaped. But no-one ever
fell in, that we remember.

It would have been a disgrace that, if
anyone's slip of a sandshoe had sent them
to splash the greenness into wetness.
We would have been surprised: halted
the game surely and then swapped looks
copied from schoolteachers, ones that said,
'I'm disappointed in you.'

SMOKE

Whiteness and brownness in her tipped cigarette
– fresh one for eleven when next-door was in.
Our mantelpiece had half-ones for later,
mottled with brown at an end
and crushed, charred, at the other.
Not like the delicate blue lines of
smoke in the Biggles books.

Brand names played a part with us.
The team on the wall tried to sound
the tobacco name from clues that
came from the team at the kerb.

You moaned against the shout
but abandoned the game to run
the message for fresh loaf.
Bread was handed over in tissue.
You prodded into smoking dough.

PROVISIONS

My father brought me on his heavy-gauge crossbar.
I came to hinder him in early evenings.
Through the backshop to the backlog of work.

Butter to be cut like cheese and wrapped
in greaseproofed paper: same stuff for bacon.
He boned collars or necks of hams;

occasionally gammons: took some from
a double hook down to be operated on.
The cutting red wheel was a traction engine.

I sniffed at clay jars for a scraping of jam.
Cheeses had a chilled crust, even under
the peeled-off scabs of strange green cloth.

Coffee and disinfectant smelled the air.
Inked scripts on plywood boxes:
tinfoil and a lot of tea in them.

My father found the weights the other night.
Toy tubs of brass in various sizes.
A far cry from digital scales.

WORKSHOP

Luminous gorse in this lane
that goes to the shore we called
'Cockle-ebb' when we ran,
released from classroom catechism.
The rim of tide did not then seem

as a dirt-line on a bath.
Pollution went untermed,
even at Geography.
When we drank our fill
we splintered bottles.

Now you have a pan to boil
in this workshop in the lane.
Rose-cups spill with rivets but
two are preserved for sugar and milk
and two for our tea.

In the once-fine room
dust is caught in broken rays.
Sharp sprays of gorse
are bohemian bright
in a milky bottle.

FRASERBURGH

The mix of smells brought me along
as if by the hand to
brand new potatoes, steaming
whole and round, by pickles,
complete ones in jars, on
a table with a tongue.

A square plate had silver biscuits.

Window blinds were of brown paper.

We were put out to
graze in the strawberries.
Sweet peas sounded good.

Older boys were in the field:
said they shot hare with slugs.

Coal was piled around the piers.
The sea smelled of herrings
in the harbour. And other

components of a smell which
takes over completely.
Things are remembered
all together. They
are their own mix.

BYNAME

Thinking of when you brought home
that Che Guevara teeshirt.
It gave you your byname:
the short 'Che' lengthened
with our local vowel.

When the batteries ran out
and rock ceased to roam with us
on Sunday streets and tracks;
while your parents were driving,
you made the omelettes.

When everything creative
was in your scullery:
packet curry on the slow plate;
hard pan of lead on the hot.
Weights moulded in clay.

The only good grace in
our fumbling growing
was when we threw sinkers,
with trailing barbs,
to take red rock cod.

TWO POEMS FOR MY MOTHER

Kitchen Garden

She would take tea down here – no biscuit –
and just the quick glance at the magazine.
All this below the kitchen window;
always with a pan left on the boil.

News Broken

You would think you wouldn't have noticed the small
    things
like the four cream-crackers: four squares with
four squares of orange cheese.
But small signs were never stronger and sounds too
in tones of voices offering cups of tea.

THRUSH BY WATER

There is no disturbance of my ripples
by tappings, even when their source
is seen as broken shells,
anvilled by a thrush.

The picturesque sound
by wave-lap
is the death of snails.

Sifting and tapping
without discord.
No jarring changes
come to sound.

END OF PATH

Someone had splashed
the brightest paint
on a broken oar,
carried it up
the path to the hill
and planted it there.

Last compass point.

Now, from that stance,
to take the swayings
of brown and green rocks and blue
in one unbroken gaze

II
SITUATIONS

ANNUNCIATION

Far from where did you come now?
You did not grow from the clay floor.
Nor did any withered drapes
hang to hide your living self.
You did not glow in any light
of waxy flame nor point in sky.
But your breath is chambered here:
yet not caught-in. It takes me
from my rest to sit and be:
only sit. Content to be.

THE PRINCE OF WALES

Hard light comes from something
more like a bowl than a shade:
naked and dangling upside down.

Edges of panels gape apart.
Veins are lost in the stained wood.
Glare comes down from the pale

ceiling to the groups and twos
and inordinate number of single ones
seated here with flat jars.

ONE A.M.

You wonder if you will play safe
when he comes up with a matted strand
of hair down over one eye
and the other eye groping out
for yours. Not demanding or begging
but wanting to say it's not dope or drink.
He needs to know that you know
you're going even twenty yards along
the tarmac way that your feet and his
are coping on.

ANDREW

His stopping of the van
brought russet and moon
as close as the windscreen.

I'd not noticed the dusk
when out on my limb:
only the going of light

and gaining, blazing of
headlamps. But now on
his chassis, under his roof,

he poised his head and sang
a ballad from out the dead,
raised from a library.

STATION CAFETERIA

She was too tired to respond.
A strain of banter would have placed
more strain on her reply.
'Milk?' she asked, after it was poured.
'No, but I'm past being fussy.'

That was all and good but
how could I hint at how
many days of missed meals,
runs around stations, rushed teashops,
scalds on tongue, it took to accept
this cafeteria with its bored brusher;
quietly moveable regular nuisance;
buyer of sausages in a bag
for his lean and sniffing Borzoi.

The tea tasted all right.
You lose the thirst for the peace
that is like a summer park
made empty by unquieting lack
of radio or ice-creams.

JEANNIE ROBERTSON MEMORIAL CONCERT

That was it, the husk, the grain-rough
soreness in the throat; catch in her
breath and ours as we played
the audience role: unsoothed
and all the richer for it.

Not a caramel trace in what she
gave and not a wheatgerm more
to mix or mottle offerings.
She communed with all, brought
us to bread under a sky.

She did not try to decorate
the hawthorn tree. Its touch of leaf
and bare-sprung thorn were there,
alive yet and catching, there.
A small hint of blossom cream.

FOR THOSE WHO CAME SOON

Tasting your offering in the dill and cinnamon
that hints of Iran.
Me thinking, not you, of the woven this and
ancient that, you left.
Now you utilise turmeric, like everyone else,
to yellow your rice.
You departed the shouting: brought principal
asset
of gentler integrity.
You breathe here now: have come to a finer
thing than exile.
Leaving your land, you live your belief,
content without saffron.

BUDDHA

Surely, I had to think, going in,
that there should be Swiss city things
more typical and topical to see
than Japanese sculptures which themselves
were only visiting short-term.

These folds knew how to come down,
not in cascades
but simply falling, circling
from the stonecalmed head and hand.

Now similar folds
are in the bended knees and coat
and in the white and brushed-back hair
of a very Zurich man
who stoops before to watch.

THERAPIST, ZURICH
(*for Ursula*)

In the hospital workers' residence
she handed me bread – a milky plait.
I saw the scattered poppy-seeds
were broken almonds baked dark.
Even the cheese disguised itself –
Emmentaler ripened in the mouth.

Her work confronted brittle minds.
She and they had pummelled dough.
Pliable stuff and elemental, sure,
so they then she had thrown it at
and sometimes through the walls.

Her work was moving her, she said,
to other wards and rooms, she said
but she had lost and maybe gained
in the baked and plaited strands.

FLASHBACK

Mudflats for the full mile at
Montrose. A sore ebb with
stranded dinghies; salmon cobbles.

The Mearns ploughed to the whins
above Johnshaven breakwater.
A standing-by rig, horizoned.

This time the pack is on a seat
instead of officially booted.
Vest, socks and jeans are clean.

Then, it was this time of year
after signposted Swiss hills
and the London magnolias.

That sleepless overnight bus:
it wasn't the jolting or heat but
the lacks in the journey before

and the fuss I'd made
because of the want for
more than we shared.

I'd resented comforts and cream,
willed for sharp citrus,
grown angry at neatness.

A retreating relief in
the untidiest travel,
to escape the curdling.

Cold that made the mouth dry
by hazy Dunnotar
and the imminence of

that out-of-term room,
part-heated by paraffin.
Over articulated traffic.

IN THE COFFEE-POT
(*for Joan*)

She teaches school in Aberchirder,
an inland easterly setting for
this orthodox Northwest girl
who sounds the play between the words.

Faithful straightness in her hair,
black in the shining sense
alluded to by mystics
but with none of their tangles.

I watched her tilt the final froth
of Stornoway cappuccino,
lift a carrier-bag or a creel;
stand presbyterian and convincing.

III
GOING NORTH

NORTH OF NORWAY

A woman who taught school here
came with me from the train
and showed me her town:
gave me apples and nuts to crunch;
made me take bread for later.
We walked by trawlers, looked to islands
and she left me in the housing scheme
on the doorstep of a man, part Lapp,
who talked of schools, good and ill,
and changes seen in territories
which were caused, he said,
by Hydro-Electric dams and stronger
forces called Economic which meant
that ranging people could fish no more
for their food and would lose
more than the red in their cheeks
and colour in costumes.

IN REYKJAVIK

That bird was like one nearer home
but its orange leg and dash were
far removed from muddy shades.
I knew no name to pin it down
so had to think of it and all
familiar foreign things, here
within an arc of the aero-stop:
long-grassed ground, potato plot,
barbless fence repaired with
improvising bits of string.
All scheming cultivation into
scarce green ground but not so
organised. You could progress
along a smiling, medium way,
devoid of litter and of borders,
made from packing-cases
stained with hybrid orange-pink
more expressive than graffiti;
far removed from muddy shades.

BELOW

The peaks were bare, confident
above the bit and piece of mist.
A gantry in haze, far below.
Hard fish sometimes hang from it.
Nothing dried or salted now
but bibbed and fashioned clothes,
too precious for spin-drying,
turned out to hope for wind.

RIDGE ABOVE LAKE MYVATN

Black and white is in the flight
of shelduck over sulphur steam.

All sneaks along the cracked red
yellow crystals of earth

to where sheep snatch the rich
of moss anemones and thyme.

Both sides are here, scrambled
up, so close to the spine.

CLIFFS AT NESKAUPSTADUR

Knee on rock, the watcher thought
of his own sensitivity to
fulmars' young, fluffed beside
clear-outlined parent bird.

He watched the compass quiver,
the adult go clean out and
fly parallels to this ledge:
then felt his own stance,
frozen, fall to sea along
with pouring cliff-spring.

The fluff breathed but stayed alone.
The parent bird kept aloof.

Then the watcher, crouching, feared
that on cliffs, in kitchens, conversations,
he sometimes sensitively interfered.

WYRE TO ROUSAY

We did not know why it was strange
to circumambulate Wyre:
tripping rubber over slate-slabs
of piled rocks then convex stones,
under piping terns and still skuas.

The ferry then lifted us across
to let us touch the Rousay shore.
We took the contour past tilled ground
to the smooth curve of once-sown grass:
a form on a chambered cairn.

We lay on top of old and new,
resting on the circumference
of that protected monument,
to view the extent of Wyre's length:
shin-bone like, stretched, but

scraped with some living ribs of fields
and the lesser bones of rafters
left behind partial exodus.
Some went further overseas than us.
We linger here only with eyes.

SANDAY ISLAND

Expansive skies
as of Dutch-masters
but these are faster:
shifting light tones.

Sea colours assault
both shores and eyes.
A lot of angry white
breaking from brilliance.

Dry dykes could never
hold that water out
so grazings and furrows are
backspaced a field-fathom.

But lichened slabs,
cemented just high enough
to make muted roofs,
stay-put on built frames.

Gales ruffle skins
of sand and walls;
of cattle and dwellings
and pass over all.

GUNSIGHTS, SANDAY

Between two lighthouse points
kittiwakes settle into nests
on two-metre, dune cliffs.

Turret-hives are further inland,
grassed over grey and fenced
with rusting barbed stretches.

Removed guns are ghosts.
Steel sights were geared seaward
or elevated towards sky.

From the placement now I sight
squat unruffled eider –
confusing light and dark.

SCAPA SHORE

Rusty red links
embedded in
variegated pink:

an ageing chain
anchored in
rock solace.

A mile on,
a blackened spine
and oak ribs:

boat's remains
at the hard end
of a drift.

IV
VARYING STATES OF GRACE

ST MALO

The swamped concrete platforms
by the silted pools. Elvers
entering with the red-moon tide.
Hitchcock lightning or maybe Chabrol,
threatening the ramparts, the keep and
slightening our sea-wood fire.

SANCTUARY

Hammock-strung nets and Paul Strand slats
on the barricaded outrig of timber.
A pretence at running blocks, working spars.

Above all this balanced decay
a high lark sends out its beacon
into an inexplicable haze.

Over a snake of blown polythene,
one drifting magpie, one planing harrier
patrol the blockade of maram grass

and sea kale that binds the dunes
before this wet mudflat desert:
this exposed sanctuary.

BORDERLANDS

i. *Mondarrain*
A slipstream moan above dead asphodel
with near-black seeds, apothecary green.

Glider and griffon-vulture eye to eye.
Aluminium flange: wind-flayed pinion.

Below these flights, Basque ponies give suck
on Pyrenees slopes. Blurred borderlands.

ii. *Contrabandier*
As faint as wear-marks on skin,
tramped traces of hooves or heels.

Backpack smuggling by the monkish
crown of beeches on Mondarrain:

more for sport than profit and
forgotten till the doctor's eye

fell on the single strap-line.
Only the right shoulder blemished

where the hand held the chafing
rope, ready for quick-release

at any winging flurry or
footfall or sensed hint.

iii. *Carcase*

The sallow tail: a metre of kelp.
Gawky legs splayed, as when it
was a resting calf, years back.

Its spinal ridge undulates. Little
left in the loose bag of hide: at
the jawbone's end, teeth touch bracken.

Focused in six metres of visibility;
dewed in the Spanish border drizzle:
is the landscape of this carcase.

I sense a tetanus radius
unrelieved by digitalis air as
I stand to watch the hollowing hooves.

iv. *Frontier*

Road-paint yellow become ochre,
nearly lichen, in fading stripes
on felled posts. Sheepbells chime.

At the broken height of sight, three
men stand by a dish and antennae:
squat sub-machine guns at hips.

The military descend in Mediaeval hats,
to mine for metal in my rucksack
and frisk me from oxters to calves

while the living noise of a lorry in
reverse gear, comes from somewhere close:
subdued signs of blocks and builders.

v. *Debris*
Enamel-white cement engrained
in the joined threes and sevens of
sections and slabs, baked and extant.

Six parallel sections show in
a regulation ventilation block,
isolated from all purpose.

The reinforcements of rusting steel
are warped to wild lines: changed
by terrorists or governments.

vi. *Pic Gora Makil*
The epic of slatings seems
cast or stabbed, hurled or
sometimes simply heaped
to make Pic Gora Makil.

I step down from strewn
summits to grave-like slabs,
placed in a circle that
speaks of people.

PIC DU MIDI D'OSSAU

Hot vibram soles on the basalt shale.
Explosive blue gentians by tight lichen knots.

A withered glaze-green and root become bone,
exposed above the aquamarine iceline.

The further sightlines of the Pyrenees system:
a monochrome forest of buttresses and javelins.

SHELTERING

Under the mustang gale that
bends the poplars roughly double
and is heat-blast treatment
to this mossed masonry:

a place of portals and public-
address. Under a simple balcony
and before the virtuoso alter,
I think back out a day and a distance

to the touch, achieved by chance,
of rough and sodden hair
and polished black horn
on a mountain ewe and lamb,

minature and intimate,
both wedged in a walnut womb,
heavy rain depressing leaves
but steaming from their backs.

After a night under an overhang
in dripping mist: my irrational eye
refusing to sleep where
my head had found a hollow.

AINHOA: GARDEN RESTAURANT

I wanted to be glad the waspish bikes
were buzzing up the one-street town:
each C.C. saying that the preservation
of period timber didn't freeze
the walls and everyone inside them.

But, as the swallows tried to trace space
between the calm distensions of
pollarded planes; and the individual
filter gave grudgingly into
the silver-mounted coffee-glass,
I only took the air: watched the swing.

ECHALER

Tool handles seasoning in the flow,
wet wood wearing white as a hand-palm.
Plain stones as weights on red clay eaves:
the Sirocco winds travel this far.

Now the geraniums are silent,
bedded outdoors in painted churns.
Car-parts occupy the blacksmith's window,
behind wrought work of Basque crosses.

We walk by without a peseta's worth of
either of their languages: apart until,
in a concrete court, the known and fast
declensions of the grammar of soccer.

OBJET TROUVÉ

A blood-orange impossibility
in the boulder lichen, below
a less false-seeming colour
in the fade of red ribbon,
hitched to the hawthorn scrub
with a military tidiness which
suggests a medal, suspended
on this scree-path marker.

The intrusion of my expectations is
a deeper disturbance than my bootprints.
The ribbon, subdued by sun and drizzle,
is ambiguous and quietly rich.
None of the lenses I carry can help:
the binocular field of view to the skyline
or the closer focus of the camera-trap.
But the sign insists on explanation.

A hill-farmer's unobtrusive emblem
to chime with other daubs of red
on a far from blatant track
I haven't the sight to see.
Or a bared flash of border-war.
There is no tooth, no claw, no bronze,
no possibility of judgement,
only a sign that's strange to me.

JUXTAPOSITION

Effortless artistry in Espelette as
the backs of hands on the balcony rail
are composed in congregational effect,
as accidental as oak,
growing to crafted shapes
and incorporated here to
truss and stress the roof
under Pic Mondarrain.

We drive to a fiasco of souvenirs
from Latinate gold to the lame
polythene transparency of camping-bottles,
labelled, in purest blue, 'Lourdes'.

The drama of juxtaposition is false.
There is oak in Lourdes, gilt in Espelette.
Hands at rest, or making wheelchairs turn.

ESTUARY AT BAYONNE

i.
Numerals overpower the script
of AZALEE and CYCLAMEN.
Operetta sailors disembark
from M-this and M-that.
Red poms on round black hats.
Patrol-boat grey but stem-green
on the visible warhead tips
and on their angled, guiding fins.

ii.
The forked kite-tail, the
finely-tuned wings, like a
long and lean, cruising kestrel.
Methodical hunger over
the drowned maple-leaf and
the swimming artichoke. While
the man on the moped goes
in varying states of grace
up the town centre with
his dismantled roach-pole.

BAYONNE CATHEDRAL

i.
The sleeping-bags piled behind slogans.
Protesters fast in the alcove sanctuary,
under the primary passion of glass
mosaics, stained and framed, Bulgarian bright;
set in lattice arches of spun stone.

Out in the town, the tax-centre is taken.
Gendarmes circle everything municipal.
the hills in the province are quiet this June.

ii.
A slim multitude of candles
composed in a stand. The
glacier wax goes off in
erosive asides before
inexorably down to make
centimetres of mountains:
white and stone-hard.
A woman with a stripey bag
and Polaroids clutched in fingers,
lights a smouldering life.

iii.
The actual carbon of combustion,
from an untidy bustle of branches.
As the sticks melt I have to think
of a book with a translated title:
'They Burn The Thistles'.
Another struggle: other setting.

And, being a watcher outside the ritual,
I remember one guide at the Dome Of The Rock,
who shifted me, as a pale outsider
still for too long. Then another
who talked me over Turkish furlongs:
a textile geometry. Travelled weft.

IN ST JEAN DE LUZ

The Falklands crisis was over, except
for the dead and the inquiry.
Scotland came close to qualifying by
driving the ball, under a temperature.
I'd heard of these before buying the *Times*.

A neighbouring negro lady softly turned
the *International Herald Tribune* sheets.
'MIT VOLLDAMPF DURCHS MITTELFELD
DANN FLANKEN, FLANKEN, FLANKEN,'
safely said the other group was German.

Iced coffee induced all observations
back, five years, to an inert island
with no traffic in the race of its tide.
That big house on Inchkenneth was
the only other place I'd had the stuff,

as handed by the saronged English wife
of a colonialist's son become
ferryman, who let himself be called
by a wind-up phone in an iron shack.
The turning outboard made a noisy wake.

Once it had been a Mitford mansion.
Now he and she were caretakers for friends.
We swam, ate crab and slowly wondered
at the carved nobility of grey over
the dead, stormbound before Iona.

V
POEMS FOR BARBARA ZIEHM

MUSHROOMS

There was nothing more narcotic
than dried tinges of dung
in the rounded mushrooms of
the Bernera machair,

or the gentle souring
of a culture in the cream
over cyclamen gills
and short trunk of stem.

The potency of their smell
healed our soreness by
filtering the undertow salt
of our unspoken turmoil,

did it so well
that now there is
incompleteness
in most I sense alone.

SHOULDER

Yours is not the sharp bone
that I've seen the sun strike

in a skeletal glint that
transmits to the keening hawk

but the broad bone with its own pulse
working on these arterial throbs

between my own still thumb
and touching wrist.

ENDS OF ROADS

You came with me to the ends of roads –
major spaces emanating out
from the terminal, tarmac turning-place:
Hushinish, Brenish, Bosta, Oronsay.

One night we froze at the Butt of Lewis
where the dependable lighthouse beam
sent regular rays to seabird wings
above the far from constant waters.

PROVIDENCE

Kippers on your breath and
the washed smell of your hair.

Providence, Strathgarry, Fiery Cross.
The Arnish light and the beacon.

Courteous signals in your tones:
your green and disarming eyes.

Golden Sheaf, Comrade, Northern Star.
A fixed navigational sequence

below the night cloud line
and October star-points.

Tensions of wind-drift and keel
in the tracings of wakes.

STRANDING

The white-sided dolphin,
like a streamlined grampus,
dead aground on torn fins.
Blood but no visible wound.
A fullness forming
behind the long marbling
on her taut belly.

Her teeth and jaw are wanted
for people who track and count
but my hand with its implements
wanting to be useful,
is unprepared for the signs
of mammalry birth.

UPPER REDDS

A caught trout in lean May
or full October
likewise cannot spawn.
He offered me the reels,
the nylon, rods, lures,
saying not to mind the date
of the official season.

But I saw the dorsals
showing vulnerable
in the feeder burns:
roe-laden trout, beating
towards the upper redds,
anal fins chafing gravels
and milt in the flood.

Not a thought but a fear,
an apprehension.
You and all your shoulder weight
in your oiled, navy jersey,
on my chest but my eyes away
to take-in the renewed airigh:
stone with a bitumen-sheeted roof
amongst the leaned-to and the fallen-over.
Further to the protracted lines
of October sunburst over an
industrial outreach of Stornoway.

You asked then for my thought as
I looked from mainly wasted walls
to a still steelyard and
the possibility of loss.

'airigh' is the Gaelic word for 'shieling'.

INFLUENCE

Rivulets on the grouse-red moor
where, weeks ago, you walked to be
only you, again, for half an hour
while I sautéd and readied food.

Now by this not-so-still life
of molluscs gasping open,
I would trust you, love, to notice
their hot drowning as well as
the painterly Dutch visual
of cayenne on blanched blues
in the worn skillet-iron. While
I send red cabbage to the oil

and only just refrain from stirring
in the bacon which you always used.
Pretences at evading influence.

LAST WEEK

In the numberless noises of
this place I've said is still,
there is your own weight
as definite as last week,
as I spoon from foil to add
to this steaming shuttle of bumps
on the slate-smooth platform
of this stove with its combinations
of dampers; and oven that was open
to take two sets of socked feet,
held out from parallel chairs.

With the sensible presence
of your relaxed arm,
its shapes as insistent
as the uplift of your breasts,
all tangible as last week,
bringing me to an unscrimped
refilling of the short pot
and firing of the fibrous peat.

EMBANKMENT

That ladder would have done in monochrome,
extending upward way beyond the useful
limits of scaffolding, bolted to the flaking sort
of railings suffragettes might have given purpose to.
But it went out at its angle to a silhouette,
over this Thames mudflat studded with glints.

A still, after Bill Brandt, might have caught
the slowed grouping you and I made in
embraced light, refracted from the Henry Moore.
If I'd been one of the many crouching
camera-holders, stalking the sculpture,
I wouldn't have missed the chance of us.

With our small strides away from all reclining,
well-lost in the whirr of ordinary costume,
we're still too involved to see how
we're not the point and scarcely in the picture
of crowd-scenes and colonial park-benches,
as mobile focus goes along in colour.

KEVELAER

You said it after I thought it:
'Christmas cockerel', long past the dawn,
after the walk in fog over neat streets
where the organised row of lamps went to fail.
There wasn't and is never a stop to the series
of streetlights, hills or clouds but a
fuzzy limitation in all lines of sight,
under the early sky or in the year that
nears the second thousand. A further
haze let the scoreboard numerals, seen
through a steam of incense and beeswax,
be part of the service, signing all to turn
to the pages as arranged. And the
practised timbre of the older priest's voice
survived the wiring and loudspeakers.

Church, for me, was *The Water Babies*
then *The Gorilla Hunters*, taken to our pew
with Dolly Mixtures which didn't crunch and
usually prevented fidgeting. Later
I was led to a Basque church, off routes,
where tall Napoleonic hats with glued-on
mirrors, were acceptable in the procession
over primitive strewings of grass. The
brass band supported the organist and helped
release a chanted passion that wasn't left to
the choir but tested roof-curves and the found
and followed its own energies out to
a square hung with petal-blood and linen.

DIE ALSTER

The eternal rounds of joggers.
We never see the batons or the changes.

    The question in *The Catcher In the Rye:*
    where do the ducks go in a frozen Central Park?

A subdued siren and fast blue lights fail
to rend this frost, coating Die Alster.

    November sea-trout broke paper-ice
    with fins, below the Bridge of Dee.

Designed dogs walk on extending leads
on the pristine cobles of Poseldorf.

CARP-PONDS

Three or five perfect scales jut
from the wet hide of a trapped carp
which gasps its mime of counted breaths.

I sense again a similar window-pool,
oxygenated and crowded, below
customary eyes in a Haifa supermarket.

I thought of other recent traps
in the Lebanon.

WALK

After Hamburg's hour for walking, a
predomination of calm lets
me enter an area of chandlery
and bond. Warehouse brickwork
towers over non-reflective canals.
Symbols say there is no anchorage here
but for a meccano crane on a
stationary raft of metals. Only
a scattering of lights and plants
in windows among still offices.
There must be people living in these
upper islands, looking over customs points
and strung wires along the water's edge.
I think of finding a bridge home to
sixty-nine and am very dimly aware
of the undemolished bunker in
the basement where the bikes now live.

BOAT BY PIER

The wetness of sound comes from underneath.
The knotted painter brings the boat's stride
up short and it needs a conscious arm
to stop the jolt against the mooring.
We laugh in the clumsy shape as
we notice this is not the North Sea.
A single sternward oar-housing
for small sculling to some sort of work
in this lake that is an island from
various degrees of city lights.
I say we are like sixteen year olds on
a Friday night that makes home unthinkable
but your irregular sway is stronger:
'Sometime we must make a baby in a boat.'

ELBE

Nolde skies and waters on the Elbe.
IALA buoyage and the speeds
of tanker, coaster and river-boat seeming
greater between these limits of width.
Delays till their wakes hit the banks
and shudder the empty caravan park
where small fertilities of shrubs
mark the claims of next season.
Ship-diesels shunt and somewhere are
hammering propellors. Sea-couplings.

IALA is an internationally accepted system of maritime buoyage.

BULLENHUSER DAMM

The flats have grown up high near
allotments in an unplanned layout
between the canals and industries.
Personal sectors have founds and encampments:
stove-pipes topped by improvised protection
from the rains that are needed by the produce.
Some plots support people all the year round.
Repeated signposts say there are designs
on these diggings, from official quarters:
but 'The City Needs Its Green Lung'.
Then you stop bothering to pedal
as the name of this street registers.
Forbidding brickwork in a school still used,
nearer security-wire and tall exhausts
than the cultivations of poplar legions.
You say, 'At least there is a plaque.'
Deep-cut lettering on gun-dull metal.
A list of numbers and nationalities, names
where possible, of children and protectors
brought from shanty laboratories
here to be killed. A cruel April
when survivors of systems were cleared
by methods which did not cost bullets.
We did not mean to pass this way.
What can we do but continue and maybe
that is as well. Though Hamburg has a monument,
erected by vandals, as a grey attempt to
grant meaning to a march in bas-relief:
'Germany has to live even if we have to die.'

Forgiveness is too mysterious to consider
and, even for us born ten years after,
forgetting can't be allowed so
permanent paint is applied to the statue,
congealed and red, random and resisting
all metropolitan cleansing campaigns.
Another layer to the sculpture.
The untidy reminder is sometimes the stronger.
Some issues shade deeper than others
and even ripple this clutter of water,
stored by the lock-keeper's house.

This poem started life in January 1983. Gabrielle Haefs, who lives in
Hamburg, writes (in July 1989): 'The war-monument is still there but
now there's an anti-war memorial beside it. They've put up signposts
explaining the history of the old memorial – the whole thing is a sort
of open-air museum now.'

UNDERCURRENTS

A logos is lit at the balance-point
of a crane which swings by deliberate degrees
far over the city fathers' hall.
Golden ship-motifs on less tall poles
are caught in an unknown source of light
storming the flagstone squares within the square.
A company's flag is active above the stalwart
menswear store and the new statue of Heine with
its surrounding arrangement of book-burners.

While the results of three nights' rain rush
the metropolitan weir and its warning light.
My vantage point is the wide window of
the vegetarian restaurant on an upper floor.
The faded weave of the tablecloth is
as green as the tabled cyclamen leaves
and the letter of the 'S' sign below,
marking the town-state's internal system
of trains above ground, serving
commuters or, historically, a
first sector of deportation.

That single graphic promises me
more meaning than it can give.
I look for more than the scenario of
a thriller set thirty-seven years after.
There's no guarantees against the frosting
of green ideas or subversive verse.
Prosperity tends to be protected.

But you must have seen my first twitches for
the spiral notepad – or the need itself –
to find the phrases which will organise
the signals a bit. Your question is
whether I can sit and be alert
without making something of it.

NOW I KNOW

Now I know the reason for being tired
is to lie with something of alertness,
us touching as our sidelong bodies
seem to want to fit.

But waking to know the tenseness of
being tired: the only partly subdued
little assertions of will to be
at work or on the move.

Until your slacker stomach stirs against
my tighter one. Your eyes pretend to peer
through thin thickets of pale hair
and home is where we are.

VI
GOING SOUTH

GOING SOUTH

After Sligachan, an impediment
deviates the van across the gradient
of the tarred basis of the Cuillin.
There are no visible constraints – no
seagoing manoevres in the Inner Sound.
But a downdraught of air-current,
speeding through isobars and gradients.

Fixed prohibitions at Kyle of Lochalsh –
backlit by a singing, penned-in sun.
Further south, jets needle the dusk,
towing lengthening deltas of vapour
over the monochrome statue of commandos,
recent poppies wreathed below their boots
– a frozen splash of concise shapes.

An incantation of Clyde-coast signs:
Greenock – Faslane; Helensburgh – Holy Loch.
I say nothing to myself as
Radio Scotland belts through the Grundig.
Dick Gaughan follows Kenneth McKellar

until border seas are ploughed – floating
a scatter of farm lights before
upland shapes where boreholes mine.

The signs, common knowledge and the unperceived
are making me tired and sentimental
and wanting to berth this van in
the very cul-de-sac I grew up in.

GALLERY TALK
(*for Hamish Henderson*)

In the lee of a pillar
built from panelling and plaster,
he played songs, reel to reel.

This was recorded in Carrara. . .
And I heard the cleft sparks;
tasted marble dust in my nostrils;

willed for a part in atonal refrain.
Remembered a Grimshader strainer-post,
bedding it in with rhythmic iron,

sinking stones round bared bark.
Taking the work spell-about but
having long lost our song.

IN THE WEST END HOTEL

Nothing burning in the hearth.
A backwall of velveteen to
the girl's form, steadying the harp.

Fingering, dynamic as a dynamo.
While an ageing poet stands by for
incantation of minority language.

There's no peat or Lothian coal but
a fiercer heat than any embers
could ever produce.

What makes lines strong?
An adolescence of energy
in a stormy co-existence

with hours of skill. But he
had greatness in inexperience.
So did the mother of this musician:

a Barra woman with a phrasing
that still vibrates the ions
from Colonsay to Cape Wrath.

Daughters re-learn instruments.
Translators disseminate signs
but not on billboards.

Outside the West End Hotel,
John Cooper Clark is the name
on walls, halls, tickets.

Yevtushenko, they say, recites in
soccer stadiums, packed with the public.
But in the wake of this bardic evening

the late-night litter-squad in
primary, quilted safety-jackets
collects cans and cartons below

floodlit military trumpeting,
to the revving monoxide
of unsilenced exhausts.

IN OXFORD

Sandstone does disintegrate in rain
as will oak eventually.
Horse-chestnut's arm is here tensed
by steel stays, in three strands.

These are not galvanised against Greenwich
or any other time, but stainless,
unsullied so far but they'll suffer
all the latitudinal seconds.

The crimps bite on the outreach and
sustain a nodding allusion
to Giacometti's art.
I stand below the belayed branch

and am disturbed in this conserved
court, where architects have
engineered their effort so
the saw has been restrained.

MOTORWAY STOP

I like being 'loved' at the end of the line,
where stainless rails float the grained tray
and the till accumulates silver, sheds tape,
as the lady with her name on a badge
says 'love' between suppers and breakfasts
and the wall-mirror shows swiss-cheese plants
blurred by the bikers who hover below
the open plan stairway which throws a tangent
of platform-glass across the lanes.
Whilst machines spin and chip and make
you wonder who is stranded and why:
the leather suiters, the servers, me,
or the migrants from smooth Volvo buses,
blinking from the dark, at the active hall.

ENGRAVER, MUDEFORD

The proximity of designer buildings
loses the channels of Avon and Stour.
This is not the sort of harbour where
you can piss against the wall,
even on pay-night.

But in one appreciating terrace,
in a 'cottage' in Estate-Agent terms,
I met a surviving Southshoreman,
young but afloat only for leisure.
The lines of his living are engraved
in minority editions. The steel core
he would like to have lead to a livelihood,
is lowered to hold in the Needles race,
offering the creepy sandeel or squid to
diminishing bass-schools; lonely brill.

There's no line on the collectable Scarborough,
once engineered in a Northern pattern,
now reeling with retrospective worth,
saved from encasement in a Brewer's alcove:
no longer countering salt with brass
but now a prayer-wheel or an icon.

A 'Scarborough' is a classic style of centre-pin reel, used for
sea-angling.

ROYAL VICTORIA HOSPITAL, BOSCOMBE

As the early iris lapse,
pale in the jug of glazed bands
of Cornish blue, against the outlook:

a steeple is dead but projects as
another stem, a bit more rigid,
even in this slatted, filtered light.

The lowground brickwork may
have been industrial, eons ago
and I'm ashamed at my trespass

outwith the Property Services style
of institutional emulsion which is
only the tint behind your labour.

The stuff of life survives or is
enhanced by the monitor and drip.
To everything there is a setting.

Here is the slithery red bean-bag
at your back, the black inhaler
in your hand. Me apart,

for all the empathy feasible to
my sex. The staff midwife is
closer to you than me but

you accept my bleary smile and
work in a seperate geography,
surveyed only by graphic contractions.
A severe gradient to your peak.

In the slack trough I am awash
beside these bricks where I escaped

and ate from a 'Menu', in jeans blue,
above type from the last of a ribbon,
utility-style, in a Boscombe cafe.

The blustery streets of memorabilia
and traders are as good as trees,
my distant love, at arms' reach

FOR SEAN DAVID

The head, sudden, at side elevation
instead of a plan, in its red
emergence. The senser gone slack,

the plot of beats per second aside
– with Sean shifted down and out
to hopefully better things.

Then settled on the other side
of where he'd grown, in
a slightly irregular way –

his back bent to your back as
beating spoons of tissue and bone.
My plural love with adhering blood.

FOR MY MOTHER

Under the head of the pewter salmon,
tail to the wind, over Christchurch priory,
I come by the out-of-season
holiday chalets, their felts exposed
to pneumatic noises of renewal,
by our hygenic nest of tiles and vinyl.

You have to heal your wild cut of
mothering, in the context of the various
cries we haven't yet deciphered.
It's not only Sean's blurr of needs
as I place a green breed of pasta
in an olive sheen that bursts

to stick me in a small slick of guilt.
A packet of lasagne stayed dry in
our kitchen press. She'd waited for me
to stir a contrast of sauces
in her high kitchen of thick broths

where sea-masts and leading lights
could be passively noticed.

SHOTTS 1985

The tenor of the roadside is damp
as I drive by the bleary pitheads
where sleet hangs about on the bings.
These wheels were seized by nothing
more newsworthy than rust,
a coal-age before this current crisis.

The vanished wires were drawn-out, long since,
to a terse whine. Core elements unlaid.
Market-forces, elusive and so excusable,
or the dogmas of a specific management:
the history is unknown to me and you –
my brother I'm seeing on my way home

through this Central Belt that's south to us.
We lived an hour, by road, from here
in a brewery town, malt stale in the air.
Sidings stilled: dead lines to outlying mines.
And, through the schooling, the discos and Saturdays,
a fermenting discord of green and blue.

We all went daft in four untidy years.
You went for the pillion of a Triumph.
I looked to greenheart in the mud of the Forth
and the last registered working sprat-boat,
no longer a full-time prospect.
A minimum of ten years after that,
Alloa ale is in fashion again
and we've both had some changes of address,
preoccupations, jobs and companions.

Now I'm hunting for a hospital signpost,
conscious of wires, ferrules, breaking-strains:
the concept of a safe working load.

VII
SKYLINE

SKYLINE

I like living with our skyline,
broken sometimes by the tractors
taking a breather of agricultural
neutral at the aluminium gate.

Irrigational diagonals send the acidic
surplus of wet down to Laxdale spate
while the unheard rumble of JCB,
Lister or Massey-Fergusson shunt

spurts the oily, exhaust escape
up the vertical of our Swedish-
framed, domestic quiet, rylock apart
from the flank of a moor.

There are easy intensities in
eyeshot of this quarter-acre site,
edged in nasturtium and thistle sprawl.
Tennessee heat through the glazing.

Remembering sleet and weeks of gales,
the flex in the roof; the drainage to do.
The planet's weather's gone off the graph.
The Channel 4 news and the liberal press.

Without belief in a great alternative,
it would take a lot to shift us now
but people have said that before,
loading furnishings onto a cart.

JANUARY 9TH

Cold iron rim around cloud:
the moon was strange tonight.
Small semblance of solidity.

Burdened branches stationary
across a throbbing gap.
A broadcast said 'eclipse'.

You wonder what portents
of potentials or sufferings
glint in a steel sky

or you read significance
in more temporal tracks
rusting into slush.

ANTON

Your work, compassionate craftsman,
I read in translation of word and place.
You doctored aside taffeta layers
to unhealing ills.

In this Westerly province
some patients still aspire
to something monumental.
Most have known love, though

fields are bogged-down while
town gates boast wrought names
of dead men. Sons exit business.
Our small samovars simmer.

AM BORD

I pretend to these extremities –
the hop bitter, I say, as catpiss;
the cheese, wedged before my very eye
from a ripe round pretending at completeness.

They're all strategic and alive on this board,
with, naturally, only a mattcoat on the grain –
the term for the table hangs in my head
from 'am bord', the 'b' an 'm',
in Primary Six Gaelic, after Arith.

Coming forward from that to the student's job,
on a sewer of course, for one week only,
when the Transit went past the abandoned table
which glimmered deal through flaking formica.

Now warped by proximity to the Proper stove
but the import of all this is even more shaky.
Let's say, between that word and this table –
all these turnings, on nothing
so regular, smoothing, as a lathe,

I thought there was something sure as a route,
more fundamental than specific domesticities
and with a foundation I'd now call dogma,
lit by a lamp as emotively smoky
as the symbol of the Scripture Union,
eastern as Aladdin, antique and exotic,
fitting into the nick of your blazer.

WALK AFTER BREAKFAST

My bacon has grown more aesthetic,
sliced by mild mustard, with an overlap
of sliced mushroom gills. Many Sundays back

the bread was white with the crust as brown
as black. Rinds were also for healthy chewing.
The tea stiffened with three spoonfuls.

An audible splatter of rain on shingle
accompanies another recollection, by that
green rise to this pebbledash buff,

on Holm Island that could be Arizona.
I'm right back in the ninepenny seats,
before the day of 'Cheyenne Autumn'.

Indians were outlines on horizons.
Wagons, like ewes with lambs at foot.
But, 'Bury my heart at Wounded Knee'.

Now the drill is down, a cable out,
to pilot-bore for the discharge jetty
for fuel to patrol the 'Atlantic Gap'.

I can no longer see an end to
even harder rain than in the song.
Only the newsworthy settings shift.

Now is not sunrise but only after-breakfast.
My dissertations on Utopias fade
in photo-litho journals, made in school.

FOR CALUM 'TENT', COASTGUARD OFFICER

Vertical rainfall hits aerials.
Interfering hiss and hum on all channels.
We won't have to water cabbages tonight.
Only way to stop the weeds growing
is to find a market for them.

The silver fellows will swim six miles
in the summer spate, black tails beating
whiteness around the black rocks –
but ready about, to shift our tack,

– the 'Ivy 'Rose', did I remember
the word passed on the flukey winds
breaking against Stornoway Harbour:
'Well, if you don't find fish with her,
you can always sell ice-cream.'
The tin-end colours made a wild scheme.

He observed her approach from the old lookout.
You didn't need that one's fishing numbers.
Passing under the Holm conglomerate.
The blind-spot had a definite duration:
the vessel dodging under your outreach.
She failed to emerge back in the fairway.

Nothing on radio. No sight of a flare
but she failed to come back into his view.
He alerted the fleet, sent the lifeboat.
they found the skipper, holding to a box.
One crewman later surfaced in a net.
The other, never.

You need your instinct as well as the switches.
the feeling that hooks you,
abaft the pectoral.

THEY KILL SHEEP

They kill sheep in their adjoining sheds:
lambs, yearlings or cast-ewes.
A section of wide ladder for this wether:
a trestle between aluminium kegs.

The stiff brush and the undiluted bleach
as ready, on concrete, as the salted pail,
the whetted knife and the all-important knot.
Sufficient window-light for clean work.

The action on the artery is tidy –
sober but fast. The only wavering
is dying nerves;
ripples in blood,
stirred to still the danger of waste.

I am a participant, involved
and yet observing ephemera –
violent refraction on October hail,
glancing on the stones and on Loch Roag.

Hardly above our studious shapes
but under the necessary rafters,
is a bare naked bulb, for no reason,
red as an accident –

a night-bulb, dim and devoid of
energy, over our butchery.
Talking and taking action cannot conceal
my tendency to detail.

CAMBERS

A wild and random camber,
on the run-down to Carishader,
brings a maritime intonation to
the progress of our chassis and wheels.

Inside the shell, life is quiet,
devoid of the sound system we failed to fix.
The engine, when turning, is taken for granted,
taking us by antennae on bungalows.

Until we're parked, jeans on stones,
spaced like curlews with casting beaks,
across the returning sea-trout migration,
delayed by the negative ebb and the lack
of weight in anticipated rain.

The thing I'm on about, under circumstances,
a mercurial hint, gone to ground,
like the gritty sandeels under these stones,

is below the cambers, the causeways,
the engineered tarmac, so far
not breached by explosive weather
or anything slyly coming in from the west.

This sense of transience I'd thought Calvinist
is getting to me, a seeping drizzle,
as the three of us, with synthetic tackle,
are spaced along the civil twilight.

CIRCUMAMBULATION
(Scarp Island)

Walking through wetness.
Denim drying on skin.
A drifted marker,

stranded, redundant,
could be from 'Strachans'.
She works the great-lines.

How many families lived
by the seaweed kilns
in the iodine reek?

On sphagnum and gneiss
a convoluted root
is bent over forwards.

A sequence I cannot see
in the fixed-wing gyrations
of the aerial colony.

I dare not walk on this sand.
Tide ruts its own sound
between Scarp and Kearstay.

MOONS

That smart white rainbow arc,
compassing the moon, is unrelated,
we say, to the halo in the ballad

and irrelevant in all but conversation
to this black spring inviting nothing
but mention of the thirteen moons
which last occurred in 'twenty-eight',
a sequence smooth as malt,

aloof above fuel, cut but pounded
by wet to dough and never baked that
year, or this. Dead hearthstones
assembling a weak curve, sat

by pneumonic and tubercular damp
which seeped through ecological structures
and left a trace on statistical columns,
now well-housed, shielded from sky.

RETURNING FROM SRON DIOBADAIL

Ridges that seemed robust and intent
on reaching sea – a recurring barrier
to the waves of frontal systems,
give up the ghost into the airlift
or fall to grace, leaving only tangible
overhangs. Sròn Ulladail, Dìobadail
or Sròn Sgort. Residual chunks must
have floated from seams or flaws,
carried into the prevailing drive –
an oversized hail of greys.

I'm setting a course to counteract drift
from the fast and hypothermic squalls
but maybe plain dead-reckoning is best
in a gale too lazy to go round me or
any wool or skin and only deflected
by these impressing Sròn.

It isn't weather that stops me short.
In the breathless still of collision
I am confronted by an upstanding housewall,
once on the lee-end but now alone
so having to take all that comes.
The thick remnant is so common that
it prompts a lying phrase:
'inevitable gable'.
I know that other scattered material,
which was shelter, didn't give up
but was shoved and burned
into the reedy fabric of this island
where, some say, Clearances didn't occur.

MOORING

Given the knowledge of sufficient
steel to anchor a cruiser,
now sunk in the sour harbour ooze
and married to an invert 'Y' of chain
to a salvaged ring of old iron
then a nylon riser to our boat –

I'm lying with you, a mile inland,
under rain that drills the roof-sheets
and storms all chinks in the flashings.
The sealed window-unit isn't.
The peats, still out, are wasting in wet.
Sean and Ben are sound, along the ridge.

There happens to be a power-cut
and there's a depth of singing height
above the weather – but we're not

moored to anything I've seen
sink or rise on a tested line.
We'll hold together tonight.

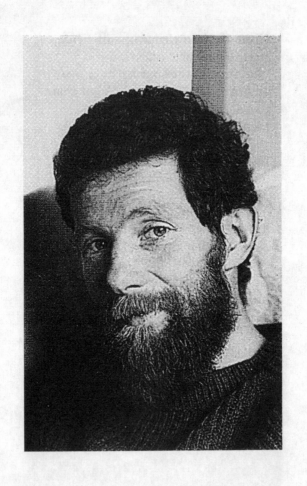